I Hope Life Treats You Well

By Terrill Martinez
Illustrated by Elsa Escoto
Editor-911 Kids

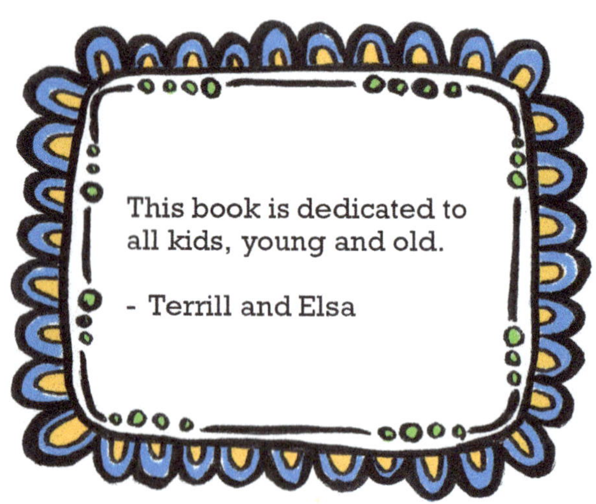

I Hope Life Treats You Well
© 2026 by Terrill Martinez

Published by Editor-911 Kids, an imprint of Editor-911 Books
St. Louis, MO
www.Editor-911.com

Cover illustrations by Elsa Escoto

ISBN: 978-1-957366-33-3
Library of Congress Control Number: 2026911455

Printed in the USA

This book was presented to

on the ocassion of

by

I hope this world treats you well.

I hope when you need a hug,
you aren't afraid to ask for one.

I hope when you feel all alone,
you can see the love and support
that surrounds you.

I hope when you need someone to care for you,
you start by caring for yourself.

I hope when you feel left out,
you remember to be your own best friend.

I hope when you need a friend,
you will have one there
because you have been a friend.

I hope when you are tempted to change
who you are to fit in with others,
you will remember and embrace
the wonderful person you already are.

I hope when you feel small,
you find the courage to be uniquely you.

I hope when you feel hurt,
you will find the tools to heal.

I hope when you are proud of yourself,
you will also be humble.

I hope when you don't have enough,
you remember to share the next time you do.

I hope that if someone is mean to you,
you learn the importance of being kind.

I hope you grow up strong,
but know when to be soft.

I hope when you feel like no one is listening,
you learn to speak up and use your voice.

I hope when you feel lost,
you discover your own way.

I hope when you feel comfortable
in your own little world,
you will make your world bigger
by traveling and meeting new people.

I hope even if the world seems ugly
and you are busy with the business of life,
you still take time to see
the beauty and magic in ordinary things.

I hope when it feels
like nothing is going your way,
they play your favorite song on the radio.

I hope you notice that when it rains,
the sun always shines again.

I hope when you feel overwhelmed,
you will take a moment and breathe
before you respond.

I hope when you are tempted
to listen only to your head,
you will listen to your heart as well.

I hope when you don't know
the answers to life's questions,
you'll let others help you find them.

I hope that when you fall,
you will find the strength to get back up again.

I hope when you are in pain
or facing hardship,
you realize that's where you grow the most.

I hope when you doubt your purpose,
the universe sends you
a sign you are ready to see.

I hope when you feel ready to give up on a dream,
you find the courage to go on.

I hope when you feel too tired to sing,
someone still hears your song.

I hope you have someone to love
and someone who loves you.
I hope you do well at whatever you do.
I hope you make all your dreams come true.
I hope all these things and more for you.

Terrill Martinez writes books that encourage kids to be who they are and to know they are loved. She is a former high school English teacher, with a degree in English and a Master of Arts in Teaching. She currently lives in Guadalajara, Mexico, with her husband and two daughters. She spends her time parenting, volunteering, and writing. She has authored seven books, including *I Am Me!* and *Even Before You Were Born*, and is always working on a new one.

Elsa Escoto is a graphic designer, visual storyteller, and artist who specializes in printmaking and whimsical illustrations. Her creations have been showcased in several exhibits and publications in Mexico and Europe. She lives in Guadalajara with her family and pets.

I Hope Life Treats You Well is the second book Elsa & Terrill have created together. Their first picture book, *The Earth Loves Me*, introduces kids to the wonders of the earth and allows them to marvel at the gift of nature.